DEVELOPING
CONFIDENCE

KEVIN GERALD

Tulsa, Oklahoma

DEVELOPING CONFIDENCE

Developing Confidence by Kevin Gerald
Published by Insight Publishing Group
8801 S. Yale, Suite 410
Tulsa, OK 74137
918-493-1718

Unless otherwise noted, Scripture quotations are from the New International Version of the Bible, copyright © 1973, 1978, 1984 by International Bible Society. Passages marked KJV are from the King James Version.Scripture quotations marked AMP are taken from *The Amplified Bible, Old Testament.* Copyright © 1965, 1987 by Zondervan Corporation. *New Testament* copyright © 1958, 1987 by the Lockman Foundation. Used by permission.

ISBN 1-930027-93-1
Library of Congress:2003103045

Printed in the United States of America

CONTENTS

CHAPTER ONE

THE RICH REWARDS OF CONFIDENCE

Studies confirm the amazing reality that everything we do as human beings we do better when we are confident. People with confidence have better health, make more money, establish long and happy marriages, stay connected to their children, and perhaps even live longer. In other words, people experience different results with confidence in their life than without it. The biblical writer states this fact to those he is addressing in Hebrews 10:35, ". . . **do not throw away your confidence, it will be richly rewarded.**" He's simply saying, "Life will be different with confidence than without it." The encouragement here is to realize that confidence maintained in the mind will produce a rich reward in our lives.

Mr. Welch of Welch's Grape Juice became one of the world's largest financial givers to mission endeavors around the world. His own success, however, was preceded by a tremendous disappointment in his life. His life's ambition had been to be a missionary in Africa. After getting married, he and his wife applied at a mission's agency; but after physical examinations, it was determined that his wife's health would not allow them to live in Africa. The young couple returned home and began helping his father in the part-time business of providing unfermented wine for church communion services. It was there in that season of setback that confidence emerged and Welch's Grape Juice was seen as a means for them to still go to Africa. They would not go as missionaries, but they would send many others not only to Africa but also all around the world. So why is it that some people are challenged by their problems and others are overwhelmed by them? The single most important distinction for those who overcome adversity is the presence of confidence in their life.

Developing Confidence

As a pastor, I talk to many people who *say they wish* that they could be more confident. They say that it is a bad experience, a difficult childhood, or a family trait that has caused them to lack confidence. Most people do not realize that confidence is something that can grow and develop within them regardless of their past. Confident people know that things can go wrong and that life can be challenging.

> *"For as he thinks in his heart, so is he..."*
>
> *Proverbs 23:7 (NKJV)*

Confident people do not deny the reality of problems; they were not all born with a silver spoon in their mouth, and they don't lead charmed lives. In fact, some grew up in negative environments and have suffered crushing setbacks at one time or another. Confidence is not a denial of reality, but rather realizing that: whatever I do in life, I can do better with confidence; and whatever I face in life, I can face better with confidence. These realizations are the basis upon which confidence is developed. It would be foolish to suggest that there is one *secret* to developing a life of confidence. What we can say, however, is that our thoughts are by far the most crucial factor in determining our level of confidence.

Wrong Thinking

There are two aspects to wrong thinking. *First, there is thinking about wrong things.* This aspect of wrong thinking is a matter of wrong focus. There is a deep tendency in nature for us to become like the most common images of our mind. If what we focus on the most worries us, we become a worrier. A person cannot be a worrier and be confident at the same time. On the other hand, if what we focus on the most causes us to be confident, there is less room for worry in our minds. On any given day in any of our lives there is something we could focus on that would weaken our confidence; and on the same day there is something we could focus on that would strengthen our confidence. *Second, there is wrong thinking about things.* This aspect of wrong thinking is a matter of having wrong concepts. Most parents remember the first time they took their child to see Santa Claus. As parents, we were excited and could not wait to put our child in the lap of this gentle, old man who represented gift giving and joy at Christmastime. The child's thought, however, was totally different and inaccurate. Before you could even put the child in Santa's lap, the child had concluded that Santa was a dangerous person who should be totally avoided. Likewise, people's concepts about God, themselves, marriage, and money are often *wrong concepts.* Again, this kind of wrong thinking causes many people to approach life from a fearful and inaccurate perspective. In extreme cases of wrong thinking, people imagine society as a hostile place where everyone is after them. People, like the infamous Unabomber, become reclusive and dysfunctional because of inaccurate concepts of the world around them. Although you may not be that extreme, it is likely that many who will read this book have inaccurate, negative assumptions about the world around them.

To help us realize the influence that our minds have on our level of confidence, let's consider three functions of the mind. *First, the mind interprets life.* When events happen, the mind searches for the reason. Our ministry produces the seventh largest passion play in the world. Every summer approximately forty thousand people attend our outdoor amphitheater to witness a two-and-a-half hour drama of the greatest story ever told. In the summer of 1992, we had planned a huge opening night concert and performance combined. Three thousand tickets were sold, and on opening day the rain was pouring down. We had to move the concert to a church building eight miles away and allow ticket holders to come to another performance. My mind was interpreting that rainy day as a *disaster*. What I did not know at that time was that the church that had opened its doors to us would be without a pastor within four months and would invite us to bring our congregation and move into their spacious facility. In hindsight, that rainy night forced people of two congregations to meet and work together, all the while having no idea that a few months later they would merge to become one church family. When the mind interprets life, it needs guiding principles of hope and faith in what is not seen. Without a mind that is *locked on* to God-inspired, confident thoughts, our interpretation of life can be discouraging. What got me through that rainy opening night was a confidence that God was in control and working everything together for my good. That interpretation was accurate in that instance and is accurate in every instance.

Second, the mind influences our behavior. The way we act is primarily a result of how we think. A person we refer to as *shy* exhibits different behavior than a person we refer to as *outgoing.* The difference in these two personalities can be traced to the thoughts, which govern social interaction. The shy person's behavior reflects a preference for being less social. In some cases, their thoughts can cause them enormous stress when social interaction is inevitable. Their nervousness can even cause an upset stomach, sweating, stuttering and tripping. Others who have different, more relaxed thoughts about social interaction will become incredibly alive, charismatic and charming in the same situation. The major fundamental difference in these two people is their confidence when placed in a social environment.

In one of the greatest Bible stories of all time, a young man named David confidently challenges a giant named Goliath to a *one-on-one fight to death.* I cannot read this story without being amazed at the behavior difference between David and the soldiers who were hiding from Goliath. Why the different behavior? It all could be traced back to thoughts of fear versus thoughts of confidence. In Psalm 27:1-3 (NIV), David spoke of his confidence:

The Lord is my light and my salvation—whom shall I fear? The Lord is the stronghold of my life—of whom shall I be afraid? When evil men advance against me to devour my flesh, when my enemies and my foes attack me, they will stumble and fall. Though an army besiege me, my heart will not fear; though war breaks out against me, even then will I be confident.

While many people acknowledge that God is powerful and all-sufficient, David personalized God's power. He proclaimed, "The Lord is my light, my salvation and the strength of my life." This was undoubtedly the key to David's strong and unwavering confidence.

Third, the mind makes choices. We make thousands of choices in our lifetime based on our interpretations. These choices include things like what we do for our hobbies, what television programs we watch, who we will be friends with, where we will go to church, what career we pursue, and how we use our money.

History tells us that Abraham Lincoln had a melancholy personality that often caused him to drift into low moods in his younger years. Along the way, some significant changes took place, and he became a much brighter and more optimistic person. He once stated that, "Most people are about as happy as they make up their mind to be." What Lincoln realized is that our minds change when we change our choice of thoughts. This same president was criticized during the Civil War for gathering his staff in the evenings and telling jokes while the nation was in a severe crisis. When condemned, he explained that this was how he kept himself from despair and rejuvenated his soul. His choice to laugh was a source of spiritual health.

"A cheerful heart is good medicine. . ."
Proverbs 17:22 (NIV)

The following chapters will give direction to your thoughts and habits of mind. My goal is not only to help you develop your confidence but also to help you remember that everything you do, you do better with confidence.

CHAPTER TWO

RECLAIMING YOUR MIND FROM NEGATIVE THOUGHTS

Negative thinking patterns come into our lives uninvited and often unnoticed. These habits of thought will affect us, our families, our careers, our future, our relationship with others, and most importantly, our concept of God. It has always amazed me how two people can see the exact same thing and interpret it differently. As we said in the previous chapter, the mind interprets life. How we allow our minds to interpret life becomes our *views of the world*, and our *views of the world* are based on our habits of thought.

Two shoe salesmen went to market their product in another country. When they arrived, one of them called the home office and said, "I'm coming home, nobody here wears shoes." The other salesman called the home office and excitedly said, "Send as many shoes as possible. Everyone here needs them." This happens every day all over the world. People approach life from totally different perspectives and get totally different results.

In 1400 B.C., there was an exodus out of Egypt. Some four million people started their journey to Canaan, the land of their dreams. It was there in this *promised land* that they would have houses, land and unlimited prosperity. The greatest challenge was *not the physical journey*. The greatest challenge was for these people, who had known slavery, to learn to think like soldiers and landowners. Although all of them could have experienced a new abundant life, only a few succeeded in breaking out of their old thinking patterns. At one point in the journey (Numbers 13), eleven of them went to spy out the land ahead of them. They all looked at the same picture, but they returned with two different interpretations. The majority saw the giants in the land and with their slave mentality, gave up on the dream. Others saw the giants but now recognized themselves as being strong and able to inhabit the land of their dreams. This is where their destinies parted. Those who lacked confidence never made it, and those with confidence experienced their dream. Recognizing negativity in your own life is the first step to a greater future.

Negativity will make inaccurate assumptions. Sometimes, following Sunday morning services at my own church, I will rush to the airport to go speak on Sunday evening in another city. There is usually no time for eating, so my assistant will have my lunch ready for me and I'll race to the airport with it in my hand. On one of these occasions, I was running extremely close to departure time, which made the ticket agent irritated. Not knowing my circumstances, he assumed that I could have arrived at the airport earlier and made life easier on him. After checking me in, he pointed to my lunch bag and said, "Next time you might want to consider not stopping at Subway sandwiches on your way to the airport!" He had inaccurately assumed that I had stopped to get a sandwich when I should have been at the airport. Negativity assumes the worst and considers it a fact.

Negativity compounds our problems. Everyone has problems. Nobody is exempt from daily opposition of some kind in their life. The real issue is not "Do you have problems?" The real issue is "How do you respond to your problems?" When negativity faces a financial problem, it will compound it until what was once only a financial problem becomes a family problem, an anger problem and a trusting-God problem. That is how negativity handles problems. Christians often speculate that all of their trouble and hardship is the work of Satan in their lives. This conclusion enables them to take no responsibility. They can blame the Devil for everything. The truth is that most people create their problems. The Devil can only be in one place at a time, and he is not always at their house!

Mike Singletary is a national football hero. He played middle linebacker for nine years with the Chicago Bears. Initially, the odds were against him becoming a success in life. His *problems* began the day he was born.

❒ Mike was born tenth of ten children and lived in a ghetto.

❒ His father, a preacher, abandoned his mother and children when Mike was young.

❒ Mike was average in size but small for the National Football League.

Today, his faith has overcome tremendous adversity, and he is a model citizen, father, and Christian. Negativity makes mountains but faith removes them.

Negativity disregards the value of FAITH. Negativity does not listen to the reasoning of positive, faith-filled thinking. People who are negative are convinced that how they think is not affecting their life one bit. They are cynical about faith teachers or motivational speakers. They never invest in books or tapes aimed at building their FAITH. These people see themselves as having little or no control over their lives or future. They see success as *luck* or a *good break* that only comes to those who are fortunate enough to have it land on them.

Jesus said, "According to your faith, will it be done to you." (Matthew 9:29). In other words, He is saying that the level of faith with which you think and reason will create your experience. This undeniable truth is obvious even in the lives of those who are bound by negativity.

Negativity hinders happiness. When forced to consider "Am I really happy?" most people think they would rather be on a beach than at work. If single, they think they would rather be married. If they have a limited budget, they think of how great it would be to win a lottery; if rich, they wonder if their friends like them only for their money. People without children think of how their life could be enriched by having children, while people with children anticipate them growing up and getting out of the house. These are the thought patterns of negativity that cause so many people to conclude that they are not happy.

When a person decides to free themselves from this negative thinking, they must realize that happiness is not determined by circumstances. *Stuff* does not make people happy or unhappy. A person can have a great family and friends but that has not proven to make people happy or unhappy. There are people who are unhappy with no children and others who are unhappy who have many children. God will enable us and give us power to be happy when we decide to be happy. Those who realize this know that happiness is a choice we can make regardless of our circumstances. Jesus encouraged people who were in less than perfect circumstances to cheer up.

❐ Matthew 9:2 – He told a paralytic to cheer up.

❐ Matthew 14:27 – He told his disciples in a storm to cheer up.

❐ John 16:33 – He reminds his disciples, *you will always have problems in this world...but **cheer up.***

Rate yourself right now on a scale of one to ten. How happy are you? What are you waiting for?

Negativity is self-centered and petty. As a pastor of a growing church, it is sometimes amazing how wrong thinking can take something as positive as church growth and turn it into a negative. Christ has called everyone to join the church but as soon as a pastor cannot fellowship with everyone, some people say, "The church is too big. I'm going to a smaller church where *everyone knows me,* and I can know everyone. After all, if the pastor can't be with me, why should I go to his church?" This self-centered, petty thinking keeps churches small and ineffective. It also causes Christians to dwell on their own selves rather than helping the pastor reach out to others in their community. Self-centeredness will hinder the power of God from entering your life. People who get caught in the clutches of self-centeredness then descend into self-pity. Self-pity will sentence you to a life of hopelessness. It is important to remember that our power to serve and lift others is the pathway to our own success.

In the 1904 World's Fair, a pastry chef from Damascus, Syria, named Ernest was not doing well with his pastry sales. However, in the booth next to him an ice cream stand had more business than they could handle. One hot day as Ernest watched, the ice cream stand ran out of bowls to serve the ice cream in. Ernest responded by running over to the ice cream stand and suggesting they serve ice cream on his folded up, wafer thin pastry called *zalabia*. Witnesses say he did not ask for anything but genuinely wanted to help the ice cream place not to lose customers. In fact, immediately he was busy making more of the *edible bowls*. The lines of customers grew, and ice cream cones became famous worldwide because one man refused to dwell on his lack of sales and decided to help someone else who needed it. Obviously, he benefited greatly and so will anyone who refuses to be trapped by self-centered thinking.

CHAPTER THREE

HOW OUR WORDS
SHAPE OUR WORLD

The world around us responds to the nature, tone, and message of our words. Other people respond to us based on what we say and how we say it. In fact, our reputation is created largely by what others hear us say. People are considered *funny, different, kind, optimistic,* or *arrogant* by the tone, nature, and message of their words. Read carefully the following truths concerning our words.

The words we speak can take us backwards or move us forward. Most of us know that we have absolutely no power to change the past. Our words and conversation, however, will determine whether or not we live looking backwards or moving forward. Ecclesiastes 7:10 instructs us: **"Do not say, 'Why were the old days better than these?' for it is not wise to ask such questions"** (NIV). The reason it is not wise to talk about yesterday being better is because when we do, we set limits on today's potential for enjoyment. Occasionally, Sheila and I will talk about a highlight or great memory in our past. We have sometimes laughed while we tell our daughter, Jodi, about something that happened years ago, but most of our conversation is about what is going on in our lives today or our plans for the future. We may talk about past vacations but not as much as future ones. We may talk about past accomplishments, but not as much as we talk about future goals. One quote I read said, "You're not old until you have more regrets than you do dreams."

The words we speak can bring suffering or healing. To "encourage" literally means to *in-courage or plant courage into another person, empowering them with boldness and confidence.* There are several ways to encourage ourselves and others, but nothing is more potent than our own words.

How many times have reckless words destroyed a relationship? How many people have lived their lives unable to shake off the negative words someone spoke about them? Those same words that caused suffering were formed in a mouth

"Reckless words pierce like a sword, but the tongue of the wise brings healing."

Proverbs 12:18

that had the potential to speak health, strength, faith, and encouragement. We usually underestimate the powerful potential we have within our mouths to lift and empower others as well as to lift and empower ourselves.

In 1012 B.C., when David was twenty-nine years old, he experienced one of his greatest setbacks. He returned from patrolling the borders of his nation (by the way, his nation was not paying him to do it; he was doing it out of his own generosity and love for others) to discover that enemy troops had destroyed or taken everything that he and his men had, including their wives and children. After the men wept, they began to speak angry words at David. They blamed him for what had happened. Without anyone to encourage him, David encouraged himself (1 Samuel 30:6). Scripture does not elaborate on how he encouraged himself, but I think it is safe to assume that *words* were a major part of it. I'm sure he spoke to himself, sang praises to God, and began to declare confidence in this negative situation. Words brought healing that day to a broken group of warriors and within a short time, they went after and recovered all they had lost. Remember, in your most difficult times your words can cause suffering, which is what David's men did to him; or your words can bring healing, which is what David did to himself and his men.

The words we speak can make or move a mountain. Words make mountains out of molehills and molehills out of mountains. We all chuckle at children and young people who focus their whole conversation around silly topics. As a parent, I often had to hold back a laugh when Jodi was so consumed by *who said what to who and who likes who but doesn't want who to know*. This was big stuff for an eleven year old. In fact, it is enough to create anxiety and stress in young people when their molehills are made into mountains. There are indicators of how God thinks and speaks found in these two verses: "**God. . . calls things that are not as though they were**" (Romans 4:17), and "**He chose . . . the things that are not to nullify the things that are**" (1 Corinthians 1:28).

Think about what these writings are revealing about God. God brings non-existent things into existence to nullify existing things. We are following God's methods when we speak new and positive things into our lives in order to replace negative things existing in our lives. Maybe you have never lived in a happy, cooperating, loving family environment. You can do what most people do and complain about your situation, or you can begin to speak happiness, cooperation, and love into existence. Perhaps you have never known what it is like to have enough money to live above the survival level of life. You can complain and make comments that confirm your lack, or you can begin to speak words of blessing and increase. As you do either of these things, you are literally calling non-existent things into your life to nullify the things that are existing in your life. The small molehill of provision grows into a mountain of prosperity and the mountain of lack shrinks until its presence is no longer visible in your life when you speak words of blessing and increase. Think of it this way . . .

❐ I can speak of negative things that exist, as though they exist; thus establishing them (not like God).

❐ I can speak of negative things that exist, as though they do not; thus denying them (not like God).

❐ I can speak of positive things that do not exist, as though they do; thus creating them (this is like God!).

The words we speak can cause our surroundings to flourish or be reduced to ruin. There is so much insecurity and competitiveness in our lives today that most people do not compliment or praise those around them. Psychologists tell us that we need to hear ten positive, affirming statements to balance one negative statement made to us. In Ephesians 4:29, we are told to *shut up* unwholesome talk and to *speak up* what will *build up.*

Do not let any unwholesome talk come out of your mouths, but only what is helpful for building others up according to their needs, that it may benefit those who listen.

Ephesians 4:29 (NIV)

Weight lifters often team up with another weight lifter. A good helper can encourage tremendously by speaking words of confidence to a partner while he or she is in the middle of a lift. Can you imagine the effect it would have on a lifter if, while they are lifting, their partner was telling them that they are weak and are going to hurt themselves? The effect would be very real. Nobody would want a partner like that! So, why is it that we often think of ourselves as good *partners* in life when we are always pointing out weaknesses?

Parents should learn how to speak words of *high value* over their children every day. Our children believe and live the confession we speak over them. This is not only true of our children but it is also true of our entire surroundings.

The words we speak can confirm or cancel God's plan for our life. Even our salvation, which was important enough for God to send His Son, can only be a reality when we confirm it with our words. If this is true in salvation, it is also true in all of God's plans for us. Sometimes I will hear a person say, "I don't believe God cares if I prosper or not." When I hear that, I know that person will not experience prosperity because they have canceled it with their words. When someone says, "I could never do that," they have just created a self-imposed limitation in their life. In Numbers 14:28, we see God reluctantly saying to negative-speaking people, *What you say is what you get.* It is important to note that God is canceling His plan to give them a better life because of their expressions of doubt and discouragement.

> *"Through the blessing of the upright a city is exalted, but by the mouth of the wicked it is destroyed."*
>
> Proverbs 11:11

"As surely as I live, declares the Lord, I will do to you the very things I heard you say."
Numbers 14:28

We put specific powers in motion by our words. Our tongues have the potential of life and death (Proverbs 18:21). If we do not guard our conversation against negativity, we will put negative powers into motion in our lives resulting in the death of God's plan for us. On the other hand, if we speak words of confidence and promise every day, we will enjoy the harvest of our mouths.

Faith Confessions
Why We Confess God's Word.

First, the confession of God's Word is for the purpose of hearing ourselves say what God has said. Some people think faith confession is going to the banker and quoting Scripture when they need a loan. Other people think it is quoting Scripture when they correct their children or are angry at their husbands. Still others confess God's Word to appear spiritual to those around them. The confession of God's Word is for our benefit so we can hear out of our own mouth what God has said.

Second, the confession of God's Word is the way we sow the seed of God's will into our lives. God's will is His Word. Things happen in us that are not God's will, such as anger, hurt, and discouragement. To bring the will of God (peace, joy, etc.) into our lives, we confess the Word of God.

Third, the confession of God's Word causes faith to increase. Confessing God's Word is like setting a thermostat to the desired temperature for the purpose of changing it. When we speak God's promises over our lives, we are raising the level of our own faith. Romans 10:17 says, "Faith comes from hearing . . ." not *faith comes by **having heard***. Notice the present tense use of *hearing*. If you limit the growth of your faith to only what you have heard, your faith will often be weak at times when confession could make it strong.

Fourth, the confession of God's word renews the mind from human perspective to God's perspective. There is an interesting device that General Motors is installing in their vehicles. It is called the On Star System. One of the features helps you to find your desired destination. If you are unsure of how to get from where you are to where you need to go, simply push a button on your phone and an On Star representative will answer. They refer to you by name and know exactly where you are located geographically. After you tell the representative where you want to go, they give you directions that are complete with street names, addresses, which way you are going and what to look for along the way. It is amazing! On one occasion, Sheila and I were taking our daughter, Jodi, to a basketball game when we realized we were going to be late if we did not get directions. After calling On Star, I got confused, reverted back to my instincts and soon had to call them back. The second time I got directions we wrote them down and then repeated them back to the On Star representative to make sure we did not lose sight of them. All three of us then concentrated on every detail of the directions together, until we arrived at the gymnasium. Often people *hear* the word but are *not* keeping it *within* them. They end up relying on their natural instincts rather than the directions given them in the Word. When we confess God's Word, it grows within us and renews our mind from our perspective to God's perspective. When we feel weak, for example, we must remind ourselves that God's perspective of us is that we are strong. Not only should we *think* of the perspective as something God sees in us, but we should *speak* it as a step of faith and agreement with Him.

Simply saying, "I am strong," out loud will heighten your awareness of the strength you have. As you repeatedly declare your strength, feelings of weakness will dissipate and be replaced with a sense of power and God-given strength.

CHAPTER FOUR

HOW YOUR SELF-IMAGE CAN HELP OR HINDER GOD'S PLAN FOR YOUR LIFE

In 1996, The well-published magazine, *Sports Illustrated,* named Tiger Woods the athlete of the year. In the magazine's feature article on Tiger, there was a speech given by Tiger's father, Earl. In this speech Earl was introducing his son to an audience, and I found it interesting that his father spoke without apology of his son's greatness. I thought in my mind about how much of Tiger's accomplishment could be linked to the confidence his father expressed in him. In the same year, *Time* magazine named David Ho their man of the year. David is the world's foremost leader in the fight against AIDS. He too, had tremendous confidence spoken over him by his father. In fact, in his native tongue his birth name meant *great one*. When David's father brought the family to America, he renamed him after the Bible character *David*. The name has proven appropriate as David Ho now takes on a Goliath-sized disease.

As I considered the high value these fathers had expressed over their sons, I was reminded of the name changing that God had initiated on several occasions in the Bible.

- ❑ Abram was renamed Abraham
- ❑ Sarai was renamed Sarah
- ❑ Jacob was renamed Israel
- ❑ Saul was renamed Paul
- ❑ Jesus gave Simon new emphasis as Simon *Peter*

Without exception, the reason for the change of names was to change the self-image of the person. God wanted them to change the way they saw themselves. The new names were a way of empowering them with a specific vision for their lives and future. Something powerful happens when the image we have of ourselves is consistent with God's thoughts about us. Jesus was not afraid to proclaim Himself as *the bread of life* or the *light of the world* because He knew who He was. It is not arrogant to recognize ourselves as having great value.

"No longer do I regard myself or any other person from a purely human point of view or natural standard of value. . ."
2 Corinthians 5:16 (Amplified)

This change in how we regard ourselves is essential to the fulfillment of God's plan for our lives. We see this repeatedly in Scripture, that a person's self-image could help or hinder God's plan. In Judges 6, Gideon's view of himself was that he was incapable and unqualified to be a leader of his people. In his conversation with an angel, the angel is addressing him as a *mighty warrior*, but Gideon obviously is struggling to see himself that way.

Moses was another man who grieved God with his inaccurate low estimate of himself. He kept saying, *I can't, I'm incapable*, but God was insistent on his qualifications to lead Israel out of Egypt. How many modern day Gideons and Moseses are being hindered from God's plan for their lives by not having an accurate, healthy self-image? What things could be different in their lives if they could only see themselves with the confidence God sees them? When Jesus told Simon, "You are now Peter," He was saying you are *a rock not a reed* (Matthew 16:18). God was saying to those whose names he changed: *Think new and better thoughts about yourself.* "Jacob" meant *deceiver* but the new name "Israel" meant *prince.* Abraham's new identification was to help him regard himself as a father to many children, and Sarah's new name gave her dignity, grace, and maturity. What kind of changes does God want to make in the way you regard yourself?

Before you can accomplish God's will for your life, you need to feel good about who you are. Below are seven things you can do to help you think and feel good about yourself.

1. Think of yourself as a person of worth and value. Challenge those tendencies to focus on your weaker areas. Offset those thoughts by concentrating on the strengths that are part of your life. Most people tend to admire gifts they don't have. If they are a mercy person, they may admire administrative people. Don't allow yourself to underestimate the value of who you are. Thank God in your prayer time for the abilities and talents He has given you and commit to fully using your potential for a good and worthwhile cause. Remind yourself that God places great value on your life, so you should too!

2. When something bad happens, accept it as an opportunity to improve yourself. Bad things do happen to good people, but things come out best for those who make the best of the outcome! Anyone who excels in a given area has had to be *stretched* and *extended* beyond mediocrity. Problems provide you with the opportunity to *stretch* yourself. When I was a youth pastor, I needed a musician but none were available, so I learned how to play the guitar. My problem caused me to improve myself and develop a new skill. Every level of progress you reach in your ministry or career will be preceded by a problem that you have solved.

3. Treat everyone you meet with great respect. We feel better about ourselves when we honor others. Although there are particular kinds of respect that come only by earning it, respect for human life and a willingness to treat others as you would like to be treated will result in self-gratification. When you treat people decently and do good to others, you will feel good about yourself.

4. Invest in yourself. It's amazing what can happen when we are willing to give ourselves the opportunity to excel. Imagine what your life would be like if you had no education. We often take for granted the many hours that were invested in our lives as children and teenagers so that we could learn reading, writing, and arithmetic. If you had been given a choice, you might not have gone to school at all or, stopped learning after high school like many Americans do.

In today's information age, it is important to keep learning and developing. Buy books and tapes, take classes, go to seminars, and buy equipment that enhances productivity. Invest in clothes that dress you for success in your career field. You are your greatest asset! The more you invest in the right tools and skills, the more you will grow as a person and the better you will feel about yourself.

5. Be a generous giver. See yourself as a *conduit* that God can use to channel resources into the Kingdom. Make a lifelong covenant to give a tithe (10 percent) of your income to God. See this tithe as your acknowledgment of God as your source. Then, above and beyond the tithe, practice the habit of being generous in:

❒ Offerings to your church and other ministries;

❒ Blessing those in need;

❒ Tipping those who serve you. Generosity has a powerful kickback of gratification.

6. Be true to God's plan for life. This has to do with your behavior and conduct. Others around you may compromise their integrity. You will see people who break their promises or are greedy. The amazing thing is that people usually try to justify their actions and excuse wrong behavior. Many people are more concerned about *who will find out* than they are with changing themselves and their behavior. There are Godly principles upon which we are to build our lives.

*Therefore, everyone who hears
these words of mine and puts
them into practice is like a wise
man who built his house on the
rock. The rain came down, the
streams rose, and the winds blew
and beat against the house; yet it
did not fall, because it had its
foundation on the rock. But everyone who hears these words of
mine and does not put them into
practice is like a foolish man who
built his house on sand. The rain
came down, the streams rose, and
the winds blew and beat against
that house, and it fell with a great
crash.*

Matthew 7:24-27

On our refrigerator at home there is a mag-
net that constantly reminds us that our
worth to God in public is who we are in pri-
vate. You cannot answer for others, but if
you want to lay your head on your pillow at

night with a clear conscience and feel good about yourself, be true to God's plan for life!

7. Put your best efforts in the things you believe in. Go for it! Expend your energy and abilities on the things you value as being important! Don't spend days doing things that you see as a waste of time! If your job does not provide you with a sense of accomplishment, consider other options. Don't spend time on petty things and neglect the things that really matter to you!

- ☐ Your family
- ☐ Your friends
- ☐ Your health
- ☐ Your ministry/church
- ☐ Your goals
- ☐ Your career

It's easy to get caught in small-talk conversations with people at work or on the phone and eat up your entire day. If you are not focused and organized, it's easy to *drift* through your weeks and accomplish very little. There is something in all of us that feels fulfilled when we extend ourselves for a worthwhile and valuable cause. Put your best effort in the things you believe in.

Discover Dignity

Sometimes, people assume that all pride is sinful. They associate pride with arrogance and conceit. However, there is a proper kind of pride. Webster's dictionary defines "dignity" as *proper pride and self-respect.* While improper pride is haughty and resists God, *dignity* is confidence established in God. That kind of confidence extends to one's self as a

> *"From the fruit of his lips a man enjoys good things... He who guards his lips, guards his life, but he who speaks rashly will come to ruin."*
>
> Proverbs 13:2, 3

special creation loved by God and empowered by God. The Apostle Paul spoke with dignity when he said, **"I can do all things through**

Him [Christ] **who gives me strength"** (Philippians 4:13 NIV).

To experience God's potential for your life, you must see yourself as a person of worth and value. Below are five keys to developing dignity:

1. Respect and take care of yourself. If you want others to respect you, then respect yourself. Take care of yourself by doing things you enjoy doing. Some people never do anything for themselves. They constantly do only what others want them to do. This will eventually lead to bad health, both mentally and physically, so discipline yourself to do the things that you know you need. For you to function at your best, you may need to be alone more frequently than your spouse. If you are by nature a *people person*, you get energy from being with people. If you are not, you get drained by being with people. Obviously, the answer is not to avoid people but to take enough time for yourself to get *recharged*. If you will notice, the majority of successful people in the world take time to exercise, vacation, and do other things for themselves. This is one of the keys to healthy, happy living. Don't feel guilty about treating yourself well! You can serve others better when you are taking care of yourself.

2. Set specific goals for yourself. Determine what you want to accomplish. Reaching a goal will increase your dignity and self-worth.

Set goals in your personal life.
❐ Daily devotion to prayer and God's word
❐ Share your faith with others more often
❐ Eat healthier
❐ Exercise regularly
❐ Be more cheerful

Set goals in your career life.
❐ Be more organized
❐ Work smarter
❐ Learn how to use a computer
❐ Be more productive
❐ Make more money

Set goals in your home life.
- ❒ Spend a definite amount of time in family fun
- ❒ Save a certain amount of money for your children's college education
- ❒ Paint the closets

3. Seek not only your own interests, but also the interests of others. When we help and bless others, we enhance our feelings of dignity. Wives can seek to know what pleases their husbands and vice versa. Parents should stay in touch with their children's interests and make time to do things they enjoy. Unselfish living has a tremendous ability to provide personal fulfillment. Please remember that this principle and the first one, *Respect and Take Care of Yourself*, go hand in hand. Don't implement one in your life without the other.

4. Align your time. What you do with your time will develop or erode dignity. Put your needs first, then your goals, then your interests. You must feel that you are accomplishing important things, or you will soon feel unproductive and frustrated. I recommend that everyone carry a Daytimer or other time management notebook and use it to manage your time. A life without management is like a car without a steering wheel!

5. Maintain dignity in your mouth. There is conversation that is conducive to dignity and there is conversation that destroys dignity. Refuse to lower yourself to *cesspool* conversation. Have enough respect for yourself not to gossip, be critical, or *bully* others with your words. Respect yourself enough to see yourself as a person who has something positive to offer others through your words. Speak words of encouragement, kindness, consideration, joy, and hope.

Dignity is essential to any society or group that esteems life and aspires to excellence. My encouragement to you is that you discover dignity and resist improper pride. You are a person of worth and value whose full potential is yet to be discovered! Don't underestimate it; strive to reach it!

CHAPTER FIVE

HOW INSECURITY AFFECTS OUR RELATIONSHIPS

The feeling of insecurity is common to everyone. Although some people experience it at a higher level of intensity, the feeling that, "I'm not OK," is something familiar to all of us. It began with the sin of Adam and Eve, which prompted their inclination to hide from God. This feeling, like every other negative instinct of our flesh, is something that God wants us to overcome. Insecurity's existence in our lives causes conflict with others and hinders our ability to enjoy positive, healthy relationships. In this chapter, we are going to look at the ways insecurity hinders relationships.

Jealousy of Other People. Oftentimes, an insecure woman will compare herself with another woman and automatically not like a woman whom she may perceive to be attractive. An insecure woman may accuse the *attractive* woman of being *stuck-up* or *dumb* before she even takes the time to know her. The real issue is one of jealousy, rooted in insecurity, when she is around the other person. A healthy, secure person will acknowledge and encourage the positive attributes of others without feeling jealous.

Suspicion of Other People. A man who is insecure may find himself often suspecting that his wife is *fooling around* on him. That thought will plague his mind without cause. The real problem is that he has such low self-esteem that he cannot accept her truly loving him and wanting him, *and only him,* as a lover and husband. Therefore, because he sees himself as not *measuring up* to other men, he is threatened. Unfortunately, when a spouse feels this way, not only do they not trust their mate but also they may falsely accuse their spouse long enough that they *create* the possibility of the extramarital affair. The innocent mate will weary of being suspect and eventually become more vulnerable to the idea.

Cynicism. A cynic believes that every good deed originates in a *self-serving* mind. For example, if you pay a cynic a compliment, they wonder why. What is your motive? Are you trying to set them up for something? If you invite a cynical person to dinner, although you may assure them there is no hidden agenda, they are not convinced. They will wonder, "What is he going to try to sell me? What kind of favor does he want now?" Overly cynical people are impossible to build relationships with because they see others as being *out to get them.*

Unhealthy Competition. Another manifestation of insecurity is constant competition with others. Those who deal with competitiveness think everything is a contest, and they try constantly to "keep up with the Joneses." Insecure people talk like this, "Well, she got a new dress, so I'm not going to church anymore until I get a new dress." Men will compare salaries, "Well, how did you do this week?" "Oh, I did pretty good. How'd you do?" When you compete with others in this manner, you are seeking from them the approval and acceptance that you are lacking to feel good about yourself.

"We do not dare to classify or compare ourselves with some who commend themselves. When they measure themselves by themselves and compare themselves with themselves, they are not wise."
2 Corinthians 10:12

For example, in a church the ushers need to be careful not to compete for individual recognition, but to excel as a group. Singers who compare themselves to others will begin to wonder who is going to sing this Sunday. They start worrying about who was chosen for the trio or duet. They think this one shouldn't sing or that one shouldn't do something else. You can almost hear it. "How come he always gets to play the bass? I can play the bass, too. How come she always teaches children's church?" As you can see, this type of comparing and competing is not something in which Christians should allow themselves to indulge.

This kind of behavior is very immature and is rooted in insecurity. It hinders an individual's ability to function with other people because they've always got something stuck in their craw. "Craw" is a word which means *that part of a chicken which digests the food.* The wrong substance going into a chicken's craw can cause serious irritation and can eventually kill the chicken. Likewise, when insecurity is deeply rooted, it will cause serious problems.

Easily Offended. Insecurity will frustrate wholesome, fulfilling association with others because people who are insecure will be easily offended. This seems to be the most prevalent attribute of insecurity. People dealing with insecurity feel slighted when someone fails to say hello while walking by. They get hurt. Nobody did anything wrong, but somebody's feelings are injured. The Bible says, **"Great peace have they who love your law, and nothing can make them stumble"** (Psalm 119:165).

When a person is insecure, they have difficulty accepting advice from others. They misunderstand when others try to help them. Eventually, secure people realize how sensitive this person is and decide that they don't want to spend time around them. It's too risky. They may say something in the wrong way, and they don't want to hurt the sensitive person's feelings.

I have seen people who were easily offended eventually end up with no friends and then be

offended that no one is their friend! It is difficult to help people with this *blind spot* because
you risk a permanent breech in your relationship with them. How do you tell a person who
is easily offended, "Don't be so touchy," without experiencing their sensitivity firsthand? It
is obvious; an overly sensitive person lives
with insecurity and is always expecting to be
offended. These people miss out on the gen-
uine, helpful input of those who truly care.
They go through life as recipients of pseudo-
communication because those who know
them realize the easily offended person can't
bear to deal with direct communication.
Consequently, the easily offended will have
less than the healthiest of relationships.

Fear of Rejection. Throughout the years of
my ministry, I've seen many people who had a
fear of getting hurt. Often we respond to that
attitude by wondering, "Why are they so
standoffish with everyone? Is it because
they're arrogant or conceited?" No, that is usually not the reason they are standing away
from the group. If we could see the truth, if we

could look into their lives, we could find that the shell around them has been built from fear. They view themselves from a very insecure perspective. The truth is: At the root of this situation lies a feeling of helplessness, weakness, and frailty. Their emotions are hurt, and they keep on hurting. That is why these people are incapable of getting close to anyone. What may be viewed as haughtiness is, in fact, a deep-seated fear of being rejected.

A person who has a fear of rejection will often approach those with whom they pursue a friendship in an aggressive manner. They don't realize they are smothering the other person. The insecure, fearful individual will try to force a friendship to happen rather than relaxing and letting it happen naturally. The reason for this is that they don't want to accept that this person may

> *"Great peace have they who love your law, and nothing can make them stumble."*
>
> Psalm 119:165
> (NIV)

not be open to a friendship with them; so they push by calling more than they should and by trying to put all their energy into a relationship with one person. A healthy person will be uncomfortable with this unnecessary aggression, and the insecure person is likely to feel rejection again. Never try to force a friendship. Relax! If it is meant to be, God will cause it to flourish in the right time.

God Wants You Whole

Rejection is so contrary to what God desires for us. God wants us to be able to say, "I can take disappointment because God has enabled me with His strength to handle it. I'm not afraid of relationships, nor am I afraid of friendships. Neither am I afraid of being alone or getting close, or of giving and receiving love. With the help of God, I'm even strong enough to take disappointment."

You see, in so much of our interaction, God wants to set us free! I'm not talking about an instantaneous liberty. In fact, that is not the plan that God has laid out–where you come to Him with all your insecurities and walk out full of confidence. You have the ability to build up your life on the Word of the Lord and in the confidence of God, in such a manner that you will not be insecure. As you establish your life in confidence, insecurity and all of its consequences will be gone.

Transcending Iniquities

The Lord is long-suffering and slow to anger, and abundant in mercy and loving-kindness, forgiving iniquity and transgression; but He will by no means clear the guilty, visiting the iniquity of the fathers upon the children, upon the third and fourth generation.
Numbers 14:18 (Amplified)

The word "iniquity" literally means *sin*. The Scripture informs us that the consequences of sin may flow to the third and fourth generation. When a man commits adultery, his children will feel the results of his sin. The longer the sin goes without repentance, the more hardship it will bring upon his children. They will experience difficulties and go through times of what appear to be unexplainable struggles. The spirit of unfaithfulness will attempt to duplicate itself in every generation.

Statistics show that daughters whose mothers are morally weak have a strong inclination to act in the same manner. When young boys whose fathers have abandoned them become adults, they often imitate their father's inability to remain faithful and committed. I've watched men live successfully with a family for years; then one day their behavior changes. They begin to act differently. They may turn to alcohol, become a workaholic, or begin an extramarital affair. Afterwards, they are sorry and say things like, "I don't know why I did this," but when they look back a generation or two, they find that those same traits existed in their relatives of previous generations. This is what the Bible means when it speaks of *visiting iniquities* on the children's children. I call this *transcending* iniquities, because they are passed down from one generation to another.

If a tendency to commit a particular kind of sin existed in your parents or relatives of previous generations, you will probably deal with the same tendency. However, if the sin was completely conquered and its power broken in a previous generation, you will be free of transcending iniquities. To the extent that your parents break the gravity-like pull of sin in their lives, they can pass on to you their freedom.

Overcoming Inherited Insecurity

Parental influence is powerful! If previous generations of your family suffered insecurity, your parents inherited it and unknowingly passed that insecurity on to you. That insecurity creates a distance between people and God. The voice of intimidation will ask a person, "Who are you to think you should even bother going to church? Who are you to think you would even bother to pray? Look at the way you live!" This voice of condemnation causes people to feel the failure associated with the sins of their ancestors. It is common for people to feel, "I'm not OK . . . others may be, but I'm not."

I am convinced that this is an attribute of our fallen nature that God wants us to overcome. We cannot live like God wants us to live while tearing ourselves down and degrading ourselves mentally. First, we have to stop putting the focus on what we perceive to be *wrong* with us. Some people are so preoccupied with what they don't like about themselves that they never celebrate the life God has given them.

Their self-talk is always rehearsing why they didn't finish school, why they don't look like a model, or why they can't get a job. Most adults who are unhappy with themselves were never affirmed by their parents. Now they lack the skills needed to affirm their own children. As a result, those children are not empowered to overcome the negativity they feel about themselves. When parents say, "You're worthless," the child will grow up believing it. If one or both parents speak degrading, negative things about a child, that child will long for parental approval even as an adult. That inner craving for a *blessing* from their parents will affect their ents adult lives causing them to always seek approval from peers, employees, friends and family. Perhaps your parents were not physically abusive, but they failed to express their

> *"...for everyone born of God overcomes the world. This is the victory that has overcome the world, even our faith."*
>
> 1 John 5:4

approval and bless you with words of affirmation and love. Today you may hunger for that feeling of security from parental approval. I encourage you to look beyond *your* parents and get your *blessing* from your Creator! Thank Him for His blessing upon your life!

> *For you created my inmost being; you knit me together in my mother's womb. I praise you because I am*

fearfully and wonderfully made; your works are wonderful, I know that full well. My frame was not hidden from you when I was made in the secret place. When I was woven together in the depths of the earth, your eyes saw my unformed body. All the days ordained for me were written in your book before one of them came to be.

Psalm 139:13-16

Overcoming Transcending Iniquities

The following steps will break the power of transcending iniquities and inherited insecurities in a person's life.

1. Be Born Again. When you experience spiritual birth, your spirit is reborn. Your physical appearance is the same, and your mind is not yet renewed, but your spirit is now born of God. This relationship with God now supersedes natural birth and is based on higher laws than laws of the flesh. Therefore,

God as your Father now empowers you to overcome inherited sin and insecurities.

2. Have an Awareness of Wellness. Many people think they are *normal* when actually they are not. Because they watched their family fight, they think every family fights. You may have grown up around anger and now you think it is normal to *blow your top* and abuse those around you. In your mind, everyone does this. Before you can break free of generational tendencies in your life, you must first see how healthy, normal people live and realize you are not well. For the record, strong feelings of insecurity, insignificance and inferiority are not normal. Consider the negative emotions and tendencies in your life that cause you repeated failure and heartache. Those emotions and tendencies can be overcome if you recognize them as being negative.

3. Reprogram your soul with higher ways and higher thoughts. There are differences in the way humans think and the *higher way* of

God's thoughts. To eliminate deep-seated inherited tendencies you must learn God's concepts and rehearse them until they become your concepts. This will transform you beyond the born-again spirit. In fact, your whole life will experience positive change as you think God's thoughts.

> *Let the wicked forsake his way and the evil man his thoughts. Let him turn to the Lord, and he will have mercy on him, and to our God, for he will freely pardon. For my thoughts are not your thoughts, neither are your ways my ways, declares the Lord. As the heavens are higher than the earth, so are my ways higher than your ways and my thoughts than your thoughts.*
> *Isaiah 55:7-9*

4. Release the healing power of forgiveness.
Forgive those who have hurt you, misled you, or neglected you. It may be a parent, relative, or even a church system. I know people who have

been made insecure because of controlling pastors who used fear tactics to manipulate them. It is always a joy to see those people come to our church and experience freedom and security.

In addition to forgiving others, you must also forgive yourself. You will never find complete confidence until you release yourself from the shame of past failure and sin. Let God's promise of forgiveness enable you to forgive yourself. Identify inherited iniquities so that you can recognize them and overcome them. Part of overcoming is the release of the healing power of forgiveness.

5. Choose to live without offense. A major key to your freedom is in your ability to not be offended. Learn to see God's development of your life in *all* that happens. You will no doubt need straight talk and correction from others if you are to break the cycle of sin and insecurity. How can this happen effectively if you get easily offended?

6. Learn emotional, mental, and spiritual maintenance. Houses, cars, even human bodies need maintenance. So why not your mind, emotions, and spirit? Take time to do the following:

- ❒ Maintain a positive attitude.
- ❒ Rehearse your new "higher thoughts."
- ❒ Pray in spiritual refreshing.
- ❒ Rest your stressed emotions.
- ❒ "Feed" your faith.
- ❒ Build yourself up.

Just because you showered yesterday doesn't mean you don't need to shower today! We often think, "It dissipates so soon, why read another inspiring book? I read one two months ago, felt good for awhile and now I'm uninspired again." Don't underestimate the value of continual maintenance if you want to stay free of powerful inherited sin and insecurities.

Inherited Blessings

We can pass along confidence and strength to our children. When parents pass on God's perspective of live and the love of God to their children, those children inherit an inner power that money cannot buy. On at least three occasions in the New Testament, Paul made reference to an apparent fear in Timothy's life. Paul knew fear was not a spirit Timothy had inherited. He also knew it was not placed there by God: **"For God hath not given us a spirit of fear; but of power, and of love, and of a sound mind"** (2 Timothy 1:7). Paul exhorted Timothy to draw on the confidence and faith he had inherited from his mother and grandmother.

"I have been reminded of your sincere faith, which first lived in your grandmother, Lois, and in your mother, Eunice, and, I am persuaded now lives in you also."
2 Timothy 1:5

In 1 Timothy 4:12, Paul made reference to another apparent insecurity in Timothy's life. He told him not to despise or count of no consequence his youth. When reading this passage, you can clearly see that Paul is trying to build up confidence in this young man. He tells him, *don't be ashamed of your youthfulness; don't worry when people talk about how young you are.* By telling him not to be ashamed of his youth, Paul was encouraging him to deal with this area of his life where he lacked confidence. He was encouraging him to build his confidence up.

When people begin to accept the value that God places on them, they will grow in their feelings of significance to God. I think this was the theme that Jesus was emphasizing in the parables of Luke 15. There are three parables that I would like you to look at:

The Lost Sheep

Suppose one of you has a hundred sheep and loses one of them. Does he not leave the ninety-nine in the open country and go after the lost sheep until he finds it? And when he finds it, he joyfully puts it on his shoulders.

Luke 15: 4-5

The Lost Coin

Or suppose a woman has ten silver coins and loses one. Does she not light a lamp, sweep the house and search carefully until she finds it? And when she finds it, she calls her friends and neighbors together and says, "Rejoice with me; I have found my lost coin."

Luke 15:8-9

The Prodigal Son

When he came to his senses, he said, "How many of my father's hired men have food to spare, and here I am starving to death! I will set out and go back to my father and say to him, 'Father, I have sinned against heaven and against you. I am no longer worthy to be called your son; make me like one of your hired men.'" So he got up and went to his father. But while he was still a long way off, his father saw him and was filled with compassion for him; he ran to his son, threw his arms around him and kissed him. The son said to him, "Father, I have sinned against heaven and against you. I am no longer worthy to be called your son." But the father said to his servants, "Quick! Bring the best robe and put it on him. Put a ring on his finger and sandals on his feet. Bring the fattened calf and kill it. Let's have a feast and celebrate. For this son of mine was dead and is alive again; he was lost and now is found." So they began to celebrate.

Luke 15:17-24

Notice that the emphasis in these verses is placed on the object or person that is **lost.** To fully understand what Jesus is saying, you have to realize that He is responding to Pharisees who criticized His time spent with average sinners. Jesus is declaring those people as being valuable and significant to God! You may make mistakes, but you are not a mistake! Build your feelings of self-worth and significance by reminding yourself that you are valuable to God.

Because we put too much emphasis on our weaknesses, we have a hard time trusting God. We have not learned to be confident in our God-given abilities. The result is that our confidence in God is affected. I can just hear some of you thinking, "Oh no, Kevin, I have confidence in God; I just don't have any confidence in myself." I want to help you understand that you cannot separate the two. By having no confidence in yourself, you have no confidence in the ability of God. That's obviously not what God wants.

The will of the Lord is that you be a person who can get along well with those around you. God wants you to experience positive, healthy rela-tionships. This begins when we are whole in our-selves. Then, and only then, are we ready to get along well with others.

CHAPTER SIX

SEEING, SAYING, SOWING AND REAPING CONFIDENCE

In 1992, I recognized the progression of a harvest in a way that I had not seen it before. Since then, this has been my confession: "What I see, is what I say. What I say, is what I sow. What I sow, is what I reap." The harvest doesn't just *show up* in our lives one day but rather it begins somewhere deep inside of us.

What you are seeing is what you choose to look at. What if I were to ask you to write down five blessings in your life, five positive things about being single (or married), or five positive things about your *significant other* (spouse)? This would require a major effort for some people, because they have not been paying any attention to those positive things.

There can be positive things all around us that we don't see, because we are not looking at them. Think about the room you are in right now. Are there objects around the room that you cannot see *without* lifting your eyes from this page and looking at them? Since you cannot see them, are they any less of a reality? Likewise, there are great and positive things all around us that we cannot see unless we look at them. Changing what we look at can ultimately change the harvest of our lives because what we *see* in our mind's eye is the beginning of the harvest process. When we focus on a weakness, it takes on a life of its own until it overrides our strengths.

Most of society assumes that the way to improvement is to concentrate on *what is wrong*. In reality, studies show that people, couples, and organizations that are most successful focus on strengths and *manage* weaknesses. These highly successful people do not ignore their weaknesses, but rather build their life on their strengths. This simple choice of selective thinking is proven to have a significant effect on our life experience. It is fair to say that the harvest of our lives begins on the picture screen of our mind. It is also accurate to think that we can change our harvest by changing what we *look* at. If something is not as you want it to be, don't focus on it as it is, but focus on it as you want it to be. Wise school teachers know that if you want to develop a child, treat them not as they are but as you want them to be. By seeing and treating a child as you want them to be, you actually begin the process of their development into the student you envision.

In Matthew 6:22, Jesus teaches that the eye is the light of the body. A few sentences later he is saying, don't *worry* about insufficiency...*look* at the birds...they even have their needs provided. He is using this principle when he says "look" at the provision of God, not at the worries of life. To change the harvest of your life, begin by changing what you are looking at.

You say what you see, and it is also what you sow. What we speak is not only a *summary* but it is also a *seed*. There is a right place to discuss your needs, disappointments, and challenges. We must remember, though, that our friend is not our counselor. To view a friendship's purpose as a way to vent problems will result in constant negative conversations with our friends. For example, some people take their work problems home through their loose conversation; then they have problems at home. Next they take their home problems to their friends and now they have friend problems. Then they take friend problems to church and end up having church problems. The reason this occurs is because, instead of *resolving* work problems, they speak loosely which results in them literally spreading their problems around. Something similar to this happened in the life of a wife and mother named Sarah (Genesis 21). Sarah observed her husband's other son, Ishmael, taunting and teasing her son, Isaac, and angrily said, "Get Ishmael and his mother, Hagar, out of our lives!" What Sarah was seeing was a reality; but could she have seen it as an opportunity rather than a threat? Rather than speaking from her anger and jealousy, could she have seen these petty moments of childhood teasing as teachable moments? By changing what she said, could she have changed the harvest? To those who don't know it, this decision by Sarah was the beginning of a conflict between the children of Ishmael and Isaac that continues to this day in the Middle East. If Sarah could have taken the high road and led a harmonious relationship between those two boys, think how much different the world would be today. Negative and idle conversation is a source of great struggle and unnecessary harvest. We can literally turn a harvest around by choosing our words as seeds chosen for an intentional harvest. Logic says, if we want tomatoes, don't plant watermelon seeds. Check the seed carefully before you speak it.

You are sowing what you are seeing and saying; this is the basis for what you will reap. The goal of every person who cares about having a desirable harvest should be to recognize a harvest by looking at a seed. If I were to want a vineyard of grapes, it would be of major importance that I be able to differentiate between grape seeds and apple seeds. Gardeners and farmers know that their future harvest depends upon them putting the right seed in the soil. When we speak our thoughts, we call it our *opinions*. Those *opinions* serve as the seeds for tomorrow's fruit. Our opinions form from the opinions of those we grew up around, our experience, what we read, and the media. If someone has a great marriage, you can guarantee that they have some valuable opinions about marriage. If someone has increased wealth, you can be sure they have some valuable opinions on earning money. On the other hand, in most of our lives there are opinions that will need to be cast down like a false idol before we can experience a positive harvest. These opinions are literal images that are ruling in the domain of our lives, forbidding new opinions the opportunity to form. For example, thousands of people are con-

> *"Stay away from a foolish man, for you will not find knowledge on his lips."*
>
> *Proverbs 14:7*

vinced that weight loss is impossible for them. They have reasoned that their genes, travel schedule, or love of food makes losing unwanted pounds impossible. I know! At thirty years old I was five feet, ten and a half inches tall, 228 pounds and frustrated. Now in my forties and 180 pounds, I have had some success at casting down the powerful feelings of despair and discouragement. This confidence came from the new opinions I formed about my ability to control what and when I eat. The opinions we have are often unspoken and occasionally hard for us to admit. However, they are visible in our behavior and indirect communication.

Since our opinions affect our lives so significantly, it is only reasonable that we would monitor them closely and guard against speaking them if they are not capable of creating a desired harvest. I especially try to stay open to any conflict between my opinions and biblical principles. If what I am thinking is not in complete harmony with God's thoughts, then my thoughts need to change. Usually this process doesn't happen all at once, but if I am willing and open, the wisdom of God changes my opinions. I look at friends who *struggle* through hardship but refuse to change their opinions. They fail to recognize the link between how they view things and the crisis they are experiencing. One of the first things I ask in a crisis is, "What needs to change?" If the engine is not running well, start by checking the oil, gas, and spark plugs until you know what change is needed. Some people seem to argue with the fuel indicator and say, "That's not the problem," when in reality, it is. These people hold on to opinions until they become *sacred cows*. The harvest they want is unattainable because of their unwillingness to change an opinion. Like a seed, the opinion determines the harvest.

What You Hear Is Important

With what kind of people do you associate? Do you hear words of affirmation and encouragement? Do you make sure that negative-speaking people are not influencing your life?

The words you hear are important. We are responsible for what goes into our hearts via our ears. You cannot develop confidence when you are hanging around discouraged, negative people. Stay away from a foolish man. Some people want to say, "But he is my friend, and I have no choice." How sincere are you about living with confidence? If your values are not the same as your friend's values, you should talk about it with them. Ask them to respect you by avoiding negative conversations.

The other ways you control what you hear are by listening to edifying radio stations, music tapes, and television programs. Some argue that you are *narrow-minded* when you limit your intake to certain television, radio programs and movies. In reality, we are all either positively or negatively affected and influenced by what we listen to. Therefore, anyone who wants to live with confidence must listen to those things that build him up. I realize that, due to the nature of life, we must all deal with situations that are not positive. However, when it comes to choosing what you hear, make a positive selection. For example, select:

❏ Uplifting, pure music
❏ Entertainment that makes you feel good about yourself
❏ Associations with encouraging, positive people

What You Say Is Important

Here is a little exercise for you this week. Count how many times you catch yourself saying, "I can't," or "I'm not able." Consider that God may be thinking, "Yes you can! I've made you more than a conqueror and equipped you to overcome!" The next time you feel battered by life, go look in the mirror and say, "I'm tough. I can take it. I can make it—in Jesus' name!"

As you speak positive words, you will feel your faith increasing in your spirit. It may seem that a word of faith is nowhere around, but the word of faith is as near as your mouth!

"But what does it say? "The word is near you; it is in your mouth and in your heart," that is, the word of faith we are proclaiming."
Romans 10:8

What you say will increase or decrease the level of your confidence. Draw the word of faith from within your heart at a level that is believable to you; form it in your mouth and experience the lifting of your confidence by speaking it. Some people speak what they wish would happen at a level they can't really believe themselves. If you are in a difficult time of your life, and someone says "How are you?" don't spill out all of your problems. Respond with words of confidence and blessing. When you

> *"Finally, brothers, whatever is true, whatever is noble, whatever is right, whatever is pure, whatever is lovely, whatever is admirable, if anything is excellent or praiseworthy, think about such things."*
>
> *Philippians 4:8 (NIV)*

cannot say, "Everything is great," you can still say some thing like: "I'm blessed," "God's good," "I'm winning," or "I'm on my way to better things." Those words will inspire and lift you, whereas the response of, "Do you really want to know?" or "Terrible!" will only depress you more. There is a time, place, and appropriate people with whom to share your challenges; however, even in those times of counsel and prayer, the word of faith should be drawn forth to do its work of encouragement. It is in your heart and in your mouth. Bring it forth!

Adjusting Your Thoughts

When given a choice of waking up tomorrow and having a gray day or a sunny day, most people would choose the day with sunshine and confidence. Unfortunately, some folks get so bogged down in negative thinking that when the situation is looking up, they are always looking down. No matter how many good things happen to them, they are always looking around the corner to see what bad thing is going to jump out at them. Until they learn to walk in confidence, they will never be a victorious Christian. They will not live with confidence unless they adjust their thoughts. If confidence and insecurity are feelings, and feelings are generated by thoughts, what should we do to get those thoughts under control?

This doesn't mean we should be careless. It simply means we don't need to be second guessing all the time. Sometimes we need to get an adjustment. If you have ever been to a chiropractor, you know what I mean. The first thing they tell you is that you are *out of alignment*. When they show you the X ray, you ask, "Wow, is that MY spine? That's MY back?" I remember the first time I looked at an X ray of my wife's back. "My Lord, they're tricking us," I thought. "They've got those crooked spine X rays in the back room, and they've brought one out and claimed that it's hers." I simply could not believe her spine really looked like that. The chiropractor told my wife, "You need an adjustment. You need to get straightened out." In similar fashion, we have to adjust our attitudes from time to time by adjusting our thoughts.

Often my daughter, Jodi, doesn't see her potential. One day she came home from a piano lesson ready to give up. "I'll never learn the song my teacher gave me today. It's so hard!" As we have learned to do, Sheila and I immediately countered her fear with confidence. We began to remind her, "Your teacher wouldn't give you anything you can't handle. Your teacher believes in you, and we believe in you. You can do it!" Repeated encouragement built her confidence and within two days she had the new song mastered. Without confidence she would have given up and not learned the new song. Did she lack the potential? No! For a short time she lacked the confidence needed to move on. We often find ourselves in a similar position. The challenge appears too great. You feel overwhelmed or inadequate. At that moment, your destiny is in question. The giant in there needs to be conquered. If you don't face today's challenges, you will never experience tomorrow's opportunities. So what will you do? I encourage you to believe.

Everything You Do, You Can Do Better with Confidence

Many people question whether or not confidence changes anything. Some see it as a *feel-*

good psychological help that has no real impact on the final outcome. You simply feel better about what you are doing while you are doing it. These people see confidence as a placebo. A placebo is something that may be used by a doctor who believes his patient has no real physical need for medication. The patient's need is strictly psychological, so the doctor prescribes a placebo. The patient thinks he is receiving medication when, in actuality, he is not. The pills he is taking contain no medicine. The patient, however, actually feels relief when taking it. So a placebo has no ability to affect one way or the other, in and of itself. I want to suggest to you that confidence is more than a placebo. A person with a lifestyle of confidence will experience different results than those without it.

- ❐ A student is a better student *when confident.*
- ❐ A nurse is a better nurse *when confident.*
- ❐ A salesperson is a better salesperson *when confident.*

Why is it that a professional, highly paid golfer can miss a three-foot putt? Why can a field goal kicker make field goals all day long in an empty stadium and miss one field goal in front of a huge crowd? We have all experienced *the choke*. All eyes were on us, and we blew it. Why? What hindered us from doing what we could have done so easily? Why did we *clam up* on that job interview and then get home and talk ninety miles an hour? We function much better, we perform much better, we communicate much better when we feel secure and confident.

> "*Everything is possible for him who believes.*"
>
> *Mark 9:23*

Your Expectations Are Powerful

Your potential for greater things is increased when you expect greater things. The couple who expects a better relationship in the future is more likely to experience it than the couple who sees themselves on shaky ground. When an overweight person expects to shed those unwanted pounds, he or she increases the possibility of it happening. Jesus promised a man named Nathaniel that he would see greater things in his future because of his own faith.

> *"Jesus said, 'You believe because I told you I saw you under the fig tree. You shall see greater things than that.'"*
> *John 1:50*

To expect and to have faith for good things in your future, you may have to retrain yourself. One lady, who had a problem of always expecting the worst, was challenged by her doctor to eliminate negative words from her vocabulary. He said to her, "Do you think you can stop using the words *can't* and *not?*" Her answer was, "I can't see why not!"

The writers Mark and James talk about the influence our expectations can have on our prayers. Let's look at the Amplified Version of Scripture for an in-depth view of their teaching:

"For this reason I am telling you, whatever you ask for in prayer, believe (trust and be confident) that it is granted to you, and you will [get it]."
Mark 11:24

Only it must be in faith that he asks with no wavering (no hesitating, no doubting). For the one who wavers (hesitates, doubts) is like the billowing surge out at sea that is blown hither and thither and tossed by the wind. For truly, let not such a person imagine that he will receive anything [he asks for] from the Lord, [For being as he is] a man of two minds (hesitating, dubious, irresolute), [he is] unstable and unreliable and uncertain about everything [he thinks, feels, decides].
James 1:6-8

Take note of the fact that these writers are emphasizing the impact that our mindset has on the final outcome of prayer.

Words describing the wrong mindset when praying:

- ❐ Wavering
- ❐ Doubting
- ❐ Irresolute
- ❐ Hesitating
- ❐ Dubious
- ❐ Uncertain

Words describing the right mindset when praying:

- ❐ Believe
- ❐ Confident
- ❐ Trust
- ❐ Faith

People mistakenly think that God is withholding the things we need and ask for because we don't measure up. THAT IS NOT THE CASE

AT ALL! Realize that God created the universe to respond to the power of faith. It is His desire to see your prayer answered, but Jesus himself, on a number of occasions, had to cleanse the atmosphere of doubt and unbelief before experiencing the answer to His prayer. What you expect when you pray can mean the difference in an answered or unanswered prayer.

My hope is that this book has equipped and inspired you to grow in godly confidence. May you know your potential as a child of God and may you learn to face every challenge with settled, undisputed confidence. As time passes and seasons of life come and go, may your confidence increase in God and His creation of you.

> *"Being confident of this, that He who began a good work in you will carry it on to completion until the day of Christ Jesus."*
>
> *Philippians 1:6*

OTHER BOOKS BY KEVIN GERALD

Forces That Form Your Future

Characteristics of a Winner

Habits / Overcoming Negative Behavior

The Proving Ground

Raising Champion Children

Pardon Me, I'm Prospering!

Author Contact Information

Kevin Gerald Communications
c/o Champions Centre, home of
Covenant Celebration Church
1819 East 72nd St.
Tacoma, WA 98404

www.kevingerald.com

NOTES

Notes

NOTES

Notes

NOTES

NOTES